HOW TO FIND A JOB IN 1 DAY

JOB SEARCH, STRATEGIES TO FIND THE JOB YOU DESIRE & INTERVIEW QUESTIONS ALL IN ONE NEAT LITTLE PACKAGE

TIMOTHY WELLS

CONTENTS

Introduction v

1. Find A Career That Fits 1
2. The Top 5 Websites To Find A Job 4
3. Mastering The Resumé 6
4. Preparing For The Interview 9
5. Business-Style: dress to impress 11
6. Establish authority with non-verbal communication 14
7. Bring This To The Interview! 16
8. Nailing The Interview Questions 19
9. Keep a Positive Mind 28

Afterword 31

INTRODUCTION

Looking for a job can be a brutal experience, or it can be an easy and fun process. This book will make it the latter and will give you a clear direction on where to start and how to cross the finish line, getting that job you desire.

First off, there are four things that need to be hammered down to be maximally successful. These include:

- Know the job you desire.
- Form a professional sounding resume
- Prepare for the interview
- Nail The Interview. Get The Job.

How do you do that?

That is exactly what this book is about! It will uncover and answer all those questions in detail so that you are totally confident and fully prepared for ANY interview. Everything you need to know is about to be revealed.

Let's get started!

1

FIND A CAREER THAT FITS

Let us begin at the end. Imagine you already have your dream job. It's the kind of job that makes you feel like you are not doing any job at all. This job makes it easy for you to get up in the morning and begin work. So, what is it?

Your answer will most probably not be the job you have right now, or else you would not have picked up this book. So, let's start there. Be it a lack of career growth, a boss who is impossible to please, or simply an inconvenient travel from home to work, there is no shame in wanting a better job for yourself. What is even more fantastic is getting the best job for you. Which job is it, then, that you most desire? Answering this question is the first step to actually getting the job.

A helpful tool in determining the answer to this is through writing. Write out two lists: YES and NO. Under the first heading, list the characteristics of your dream job. These items can range from practical matters such as: location, work hours, salary and company benefits, and even dress code. They could also be more personal issues like creative freedom, culture fit, and corporate ethics.

Under the second, list the things you would not like in a job. If you are unsatisfied with your current job, you could write in this list the reasons for your dissatisfaction and unhappiness at work right now. From these two lists, you will be able to narrow down your possible career options to more specific work, and eventually to specific companies that fit your requirements.

Now, make a list of potential companies to work. You would have to do further research in order to ensure that these companies do indeed fit your criteria. Moreover, knowing more about these companies and the industries you wish to work for would prove useful in future job applications and interviews. In your research, also include the contact details (e.g., contact person, phone numbers, e-mail addresses, and mailing addresses) of their Human Resources Department, as well as the potential hiring managers of the departments you are currently eyeing. These details and pieces of information will come in handy later on.

The most convenient way to find them is through the Internet. Any respectable company or institution would have some form of online presence like a website with a paid domain name, a social networking page, or just a simple listing in an online business directory. Otherwise, you can go to traditional means, and scan through the telephone book under the headings relevant to your desired profession.

You can also search the classified ads in your local newspaper. At this point, it would also be prudent to sign up for an account with a job hunting website which will allow you to have access to thousands of legitimate job listings, and also allow prospective employers to seek you out personally according to your credentials. Such websites would help you get in contact with head hunters and employment agencies, which could make your job hunting easier by matching you up with companies that suit your specific requirements. Right now, it is important to have the courage to admit that you need a new job, and to actually take the right steps toward finding the best one.

While searching for jobs you would like to apply for, make sure to have an updated resumé on hand. The next section will tackle this topic further. I encourage you to complete this within 3 days to keep on track with the 21-Day Formula. If you get it done sooner, that's great! Just keep moving forward with the next steps.

2
THE TOP 5 WEBSITES TO FIND A JOB

First off, if you don't already have a LinkedIn account, get one because it is an excellent free resource to connect with colleagues, friends, and other people in your industry of choice. You've probably heard that "it's not what you know, it's who you know." Therefore, it is important to join and be active on LinkedIn, and connect or reconnect with people you haven't contacted for a while or maybe someone new. It's not guaranteed that you'll get a response back. Although, if it's someone you already know, chances are they will be happy to hear from you and will be more likely to help you out or connect you to people that can get you in with the right people for the job you desire. To connect now, go to **LinkedIn.** Following, are the top 5 websites to find a job.

1. **Glassdoor** lets you enter using your Facebook account through Facebook Business Networking. It view the latest job listings as well as the salary reports, employee ratings and reviews, and company videos.

. . .

2. **CareerBuilder** has made some significant improvements over the past few years. It has become very user friendly and allows you to search using a mobile app. There is also an option to have emails sent to you as jobs are posted.

3. **Indeed** has become one of the most popular ways to find a job. It allows you to search by location, experience, salary, or industry. It lets you track job listings such as: newspaper classifieds, company career pages and job boards. One of the things that differentiates this site is that you can read what past employees thought about their job. You can also have new job listings sent to you via email.

4. **Job-Hunt** focuses on job seekers over the age of 50. It is an excellent resource because it also allows you to directly connect to LinkedIn to search for job listings. It also has a search tab where you can type in the job you're looking for and it will give you a list of qualified jobs near you. It is also easy to use.

5. **Encore** is the best place to search for second careers in nonprofits. It links to various non-profit sites and job boards, as well as over 5 million job-listings on its own site.

3
MASTERING THE RESUMÉ

Let us first take a look at your resumé on the surface. It should **look professional and be well-written.** If you have no clue what that means, then try looking at samples of good resumés uploaded on the web. See how these resumés are formatted and laid-out. Look at **how information is organized** and written in ways that are **easy to understand for the reader.** Also, try to **get a feel of the kind of language** employed in writing resumés. Notice what strong keywords or terms are commonly used by applicants in the industry you wish to work in.

Remember that you will be judged first through your resumé, so it is best to **give a very good and professional first impression** to your prospective employer. Otherwise, hiring managers would not even bother to peruse your credentials and other application requirements and see if you are actually qualified for the job. Also, the actual resumé itself should look proper. Nothing else says unprofessional like a resumé printed on pink scented paper! You might think that it is creative and would make you stand out. You will, but for all the wrong reasons. Just choose to **print on clean white paper of good stock.**

There are different types of resumés that you can write. It will **depend on the specific job you are applying for**, the requirement of the company, and your own personal situation. One basic type of resumé is a **chronological resumé**, which lists your work experience in sequence, conventionally beginning with your recent employment. Another type of resumé is a **functional resumé**, which lists your skills and professional abilities in the order of importance or relevance.

It would be good to **be familiar with the job description** of the work you are applying for, and write your resumé with the salient points of that description in mind. There are resumé templates that you can download online, or come bundled with word processing software applications. These usually prove useful as guides in crafting your own resumé. But, you can still tweak them to better suit your specific context.

Furthermore, **keep your resumé comprehensive yet concise.** Brevity here is the key because a hiring manager has no time to read a very long-winded description of all your achievements. Explaining and clarifying certain points made in your resumé is what the job interview is for. Thus, it is important to be certain of all the information written in your resumé. It would also definitely be best that you **write your resumé yourself,** and not ask someone else to do it for you. This is crucial in understanding every item mentioned in your resumé, and preparing yourself to elucidate or justify anything you have written if it happens to come up during the interview.

Also, **do not write any incorrect or misleading information.** These details could possibly be checked by hiring managers who have the means to access certain corporate data. An inaccurate item could invalidate your entire resumé and discredit you in the eyes of your prospective employer.

Creative resumés are useful among job hunters, but that does not mean that these are always effective. A resumé in an unconventional format or unusual medium is usually more suited for applications to creative jobs such as with advertising agencies, publications, or entertainment production companies. However, an overly artistic resumé which is difficult to read and store in a desk drawer, does not translate well into a photocopy, or even shows the applicant's lack of restraint, taste, and basic layout skills could terribly backfire.

What you should do is explore simple typography, incorporate a terrific but minimalist graphic illustration, or just have a very inventive outline that will make your resumé stand out, and become memorable from a sea of bland application requirements. Make sure that it also shows your professional side.

Complete this by the end of day 5, and lets keep moving forward by preparing for "The Job Interview".

4

PREPARING FOR THE INTERVIEW

When preparing for job interviews, most applicants would just focus on the actual interview—the questions and answers shared back and forth between the interviewer and the potential employee. We will eventually get to that in this section, but first, you must not overlook the other aspects of the interview.

One factor which could make or break the interview is **you**, or rather the you which you are presenting to your future boss. If your resumé serves as your first impression, then **a call for an interview means that the hiring manager was indeed impressed with the person you are on paper.** So, if this accomplished and highly qualified individual in the resumé does not match what he or she now sees in front of him, then the interview is off to a bad start. Now, what are the ways in which you could disillusion the hiring manager?

First, **be mindful of how you look on the surface.** Notice if your attire is suited for the job and the workplace. There are jobs that prescribe corporate business attire, while others are more lenient and allow smart casual clothing. Also, check if your clothes are wrinkled, and need a run with a steamer before leaving the house. Look at your shoes to check for dirt and if they need a bit of polishing. Make sure that your socks match and your necktie is not askew.

For the ladies, check your stockings for runs and even your nail polish for chippings. Look yourself over from head to toe in the mirror to see if you probably need a comb, a shave, and if you are female, a retouch on the makeup. It is understandable that you would be quite rattled on the day of the interview, but that is definitely not an excuse to be sloppy with your appearance. **It is easier to believe that a person has had a successful career, and is destined for excellence if he or she is dressed the part.**

These same guidelines also apply, even if you are being interviewed online via webcam. Additionally, it would be good to make sure that you have a good, uncluttered background. If you could set up a space that looks like an office—even if you do not really have one—then that would be better. Also, make sure to **block all external noise and other distractions** that could disturb the proceedings of your interview. This also applies to phone interviews.

5

BUSINESS-STYLE: DRESS TO IMPRESS

With just one glance, our clothes deliver our position in life. How we present ourselves also shows how much we value every meeting whether it may be formal or not. A lack of quality how kept and what style of clothes you wear may cause people to have less respect for you. For example, what do you think a new business client would think of you if you introduced yourself wearing a wrinkled t-shirt and dirty old untied shoes on?

However, be careful when choosing a classic polo and coat that are common. Although they do create a sense of credibility, you can't afford to be blurred out in the background. Choose a polo shirt and a stylish business coat to accompany it. Solid colors are usually preferred over eye-distracting designs. Also, choose a necktie that will compliment your polo to create two colors that standout among each other.

WOMEN, on the other hand, can express themselves more

freely by wearing dresses. Just make sure that your clothes are appropriate. Check the neckline and backside of your clothes if they are revealing too much skin.

If the meeting is informal, wear semi-casuals. Wearing semi-casuals deliver an outgoing but serious aura. Never settle for t-shirts. In some companies, wearing clothes like those are disrespectful.

Black straight cut pants are the norm for bottoms. Women usually wear pencil skirts that are 3 inches above the knee. Jeans are never advisable unless the meeting is informal. However, shorts are highly discouraged.

Your choice of footwear also matters. Make sure to properly care for your shoes frequently because people associate shoes with wealth and status. A poorly maintained pair of shoes creates a bad first impression. Women are recommended to wear heels at least 1 inch high. Above all else, never wear slippers or flip-flops even if it is a casual meeting.

The Power of the first handshake

Never underestimate the power of a handshake. Handshakes are a symbol of goodwill and agreement, but it can also be used to send a strong subliminal message of authority.

There are three kinds of handshakes.

1. The dominant handshake that uses the palm-facing downwards to create an impression of authority. Use the dominant handshake in meetings that have a crucial agenda where the decision will either benefit or damage your firm.

While, the submissive handshake delivers the opposite

message with the palm faced upward. It is never recommended to use the submissive handshake because you need to lead people and not the other way around.

And the standard handshake creates a sense of equality between two people by making both hands hold in the same manner. Make a standard handshake when you meet customers and clients to imply that you are both in the same level. This also helps make you appear approachable to people. After sealing a deal, use the standard handshake again to send a message of satisfaction.

Make your handshakes firm and warm. A firm handshake is a sign of confidence and power. In the US, women shake their hands only by holding the edge of the fingers. However, women in business don't. They still prefer the classic business shake. Holding on to the edge of the hand will make people think that their hands are dirty or you don't like them at all.

Time the handshakes well. Simply hold and pump the hands three times in an up-down motion. You can further reinforce friendship by using the other hand to slightly hold the shoulder, elbow or forearm of your partner. Finally, while you shake hands, make it sincere by brightly smiling at them. Although handshakes are a small gesture that happens only in 5 seconds, it creates positive energy both at the beginning and ending of meetings.

6

ESTABLISH AUTHORITY WITH NON-VERBAL COMMUNICATION

In the business world, not only do we need to create trust, we also need to build authority. Our behavior during a meeting speaks a lot about how credible and confident we are. A good show of body language can affect your sales and even job position.

Your posture and height are the one of the few things that people notice. People who are tall and stand straight are associated as being confident. This is highly important in business especially when dealing with clients. Posture creates positive energy that you are not burdened with problems. Straight posture can further add authority if your chin is slightly pointing upward and your chest is projected outward.

People get influenced easily if you speak to them while looking in their eyes. This conveys an image of seriousness and adds credibility to your message. Be mindful that you should look in a person's eyes only 60% of the time. Any more than this will intimidate your client. Use the other 40% looking at random areas beside the eye to ease tension.

While walking exude confidence and authority by

swinging your arms in a firm manner. Make every action precise. Eloquence while moving make it appear that you don't make mistakes and that you calculate every movement.

Previously, we discussed the Merkel Rhombus, which is a hand gesture created by holding your hands together and forming a triangle, and then slightly moving the thumbs toward you to make a rhombus shape. The Merkel Rhombus is a new gesture that symbolizes a calm but serious behavior. Using this body language will make you approachable at the same time respected.

THE MERKEL RHOMBUS goes well with a firm and soft voice. People tend to listen more closely to a soft but audible voice rather than a loud one. A slow rhythm will make every person cling on to your every word. Just be careful not to speak too slowly because people might lose interest in you.

While standing up, take note of your feet. You might be appearing confident from the waist up, but if your legs won't lose their nerves, they'll make it obvious. Counter this by slightly opening your legs and creating a 45 degree angle between them. Refrain from moving because it might bring back your anxiety and soon you'll be shaking again.

Contrary to popular belief, putting your hands on your waist is not a sign of felinity. In fact, male executives do this gesture more than women, for you make it appear that you are calm and relaxed in the face of stressful activities.

Combining these non-verbal authoritative cues to gestures that establish rapport will help you become an effective businessman. Non-verbal communication greatly increases your charisma that persuades people to agree to you.

7

BRING THIS TO THE INTERVIEW!

Furthermore, if going to a personal interview, do not leave your house without the usual job interview requisites. **Bring the resumé** which we have worked on in the last chapter. Have enough copies on hand for yourself and for the interview, **plus extra copies**, should you be asked for more. Make sure to also **bring your list of references with their complete contact information**.

Also **bring along with you a notebook, a smartphone, or a tablet**—whichever is more comfortable for you to take notes on—with your notes on the details of the job interview itself. This would include the interviewer's name, the address of the venue, and other information relevant to the interview. In addition, remember to bring along any other application requirements that were asked from you.

A last reminder before the actual interview itself is to **avoid being late for the appointment.** Tardiness is universally seen as unprofessional and irresponsible. These are two characteristics that you do not wish to project during a job interview.

During your interview, it is important to **show the**

prospective employer how you can be an asset to the company. Show them that hiring you is a great investment that would eventually yield impressive returns. Although it is true that you chose to apply for a job at the company because it will benefit you in many different ways, do not make the employer feel that hiring you is a one-sided deal. Make the employer understand that **it would be an honor to work for the company**. However, do not focus so much on what you would gain in return—business connections, out-of-town trips, good salary and benefits, or enough experience so you can move on to an even better job. Saying these will make one appear selfish and a risky employee to hire.

Also, **be specific when answering your interviewer.** Vague or broad answers show inexperience or lack of knowledge in the topic or work aspect. **Provide details and real life examples** to justify your claims. If possible, cite actual names or figures (if they are impressive) to support your answers. For example, if you are applying for an advertising agency, then it would be good to share which advertisements or commercials you have worked on, especially if these are popular ones.

Also, citing the exact percentage increase or sales growth in dollars would make your claims sound even more striking, and also show how truly involved you were with your former work. Although, be wary of disclosing any information which your former employers asked you to keep confidential. Revealing these to the interviewer might indicate to him or her that you are untrustworthy and would likewise not be able to keep any private corporate information, which you might acquire under your employment.

At the end of the job interview, you would most certainly be asked if you have any questions for your interviewer. Saying that you do not have any questions indicates that you were disinterested throughout the interview, would like to get it over with, and not attracted to work with the company. Instead, **think of questions that show that you are interested in the work** that the company does, and reveals that you have done some background research or have stock knowledge on the company and the industry as a whole.

You can even prepare these questions beforehand. Also, ask questions that would allow you to validate the list you made in Chapter 1. Is this really the job you desire? Although at this point, it does not seem courteous to ask about the salary and company benefits. You will usually be informed about this matter during the negotiation phase, when they are already considering you for the position.

If you encounter the nerves in the process of your interview, do not find this such a bad thing. It simply means that you care enough about the job to be nervous about it. What you can do is to prepare. It might be quite a humbling experience to prepare for a job interview by going through possible questions and rehearsing the answers. Doing so is not a sign of an incompetent interviewee. Even all the best public speakers and speech-makers rehearse their lines, and so should you. To get your dream job, you must be willing to go the extra mile.

Lastly, **enjoy your interview.** Just **relax and take it easy because the interview is really just all about you**—a topic you know by heart. The job interviewer might certainly be intimidating, but if you show that you are qualified, then he or she will not be so uptight especially if the interviewer has already decided that you would make a great addition to the company.

8

NAILING THE INTERVIEW QUESTIONS

This chapter will discuss questions that are usually asked during job interviews; and how you can answer them successfully.

1. Could you tell me about yourself?

This is usually the first thing interviewers ask at job interviews. **Have a short elevator speech about yourself,** which already tells your background, qualifications and a bit about your character. Think of it as a sales pitch. A good salesman will go about his speech quickly, before his prospect client had a chance to turn away or close the door at him. But in these 30 seconds, he has effectively said his product's amazing features, benefits and unique selling points, thereby capturing his audience's attention and making them want to know his product even further. Try not to pre-empt any further questions, which the interview would subsequently ask. Therefore, **keep your speech simple and be straight to the point.**

. . .

2. When working on a particular project, are you a team player or are you better working independently?

This is an interesting trick question. Answer one, and it shows that you are lacking in the other. If you say that you are a team player, then you are saying that you work well with others and are essentially a good collaborator. However, it also shows that you cannot work by yourself and would need constant supervision in order to finish a task properly; you would need people to always be helping you with your job.

On the other hand, if you say that you like being independent, then you are saying that you are self-sufficient and have self-initiative. Nonetheless, it as well shows that you like being autonomous and do not play well with others. You might not like listening to others' opinions and value your own ideas the most; you would be a liability in a department or team setup. Thus, **answer that you are both**. Everyone is, in some way, a bit of both. Say that you well work with a team and like sharing and brainstorming ideas with others, but when left to your own devices, you can also shine and produce quality output.

3. Are you a leader or a follower?

Similar to the question posed previously, this is another trick question which you must have a "both" answer to. State the qualities of a good leader and how you possess those qualities. Show how you were able to, in the past, steer your team towards setting goals and achieving success. Also, state the qualities of a good follower and how you are such. Show that you are still able to respect authority—possibly the interviewer's authority—and can follow directions that you have been given.

. . .

4. What is the biggest mistake you have done in your previous work?

Everyone has mistakes, so never admit to not having any. State mistakes that are general and most people have encountered, like an unsatisfied buyer at the old store which you worked at. Say how you handled the situation and what you learned from that mistake. Show that you have grown as a person due to these mistakes. State mistakes in a way that do not show that you are lacking in ability, or unable to do your job properly.

5. What are your goals in life?

A staple in job interviews, many employees have heard this question several times, and yet this may be one of the most difficult to answer. What hiring managers are looking for here is a person's ability to plan and a display of ambition. When stating your goals one, five or ten years from now, make sure that you also elaborate your personal plan of action in order to achieve these goals. Do not simply say your goals and not know how to go about accomplishing them.

Also, have goals for every aspect of your life—career, family and personal growth. State what career achievement is for you, and in what position you see yourself in the future. Say what you wish to have accomplished in your family life at a certain point in time. If you have any personal side projects like being a certified yoga instructor or travelling the entire world's continents before you turn a certain age, then mention those, too.

. . .

6. I think you are overqualified

Though this statement is not exactly posed as a question, it still in a way asks: Why should I still hire you even if you are overqualified? As flattering as it may be, being told that you are overqualified is not something you would like to hear. Employers who view you as overqualified might perceive you as someone who would eventually think that you are too good for their company and subsequently move on to better and greener pastures.

In this case, you can say that if indeed your qualifications and skills make you overqualified for the job, then that is a good thing. They would be making a great long-term investment in you. With your skills, you will also be able to help take the company to another level of success.

7. What motivates you?

Your answer to this gives the hiring manager **a clearer idea of your work ethics** and **how you would function in the company**. When asked about your motivations, what inspires you, and your driving force to do your best, give a very sincere and open answer that is relevant to the work that you are applying for. A safe answer would be that the drive to accomplish goals comes from the sense of achievement which you will eventually enjoy at the end of every successful project.

Another good answer would be having the desire to contribute to the betterment and improvement of the company is what will make you go the extra mile, and do just a little bit more every day at work. You may also give your personal motivations to give your answer a more human touch. A great motivation for most people is being able to provide the very best, and being a great person for their family—working hard so that you would be able to send all your children to college, giving your brothers and sisters a role model to look up to, and making your parents proud of the person you have become.

A desire to achieve more in life and making something important of oneself is also a motivation for most people. Whatever you say your motivations may be, **keep them positive** and almost noble. Do not state motivations that may be viewed as negative—no matter how true they may be. A lot of money, however highly motivating to most, is not good to mention as one of your motivators in work and in life.

8. How do you cope with stress?

The hiring manager might also be interested in knowing how well you cope with negative or stress-filled situations. The answer to this question actually is dependent on the specific person. Some people actually enjoy stress, for this allows them to work even better. These people probably like moving at a fast-paced environment, and are quick to react to certain situations. They also possess very good decision-making skills.

Other people tend to avoid stress by reacting properly to certain situations. They handle the problem rather than making a big, stressful deal about it. They are good with prioritizing, and they focus on the more important matters at hand, rather than the little stressors.

Others just find a release to everyday work stress by doing rigorous sports or unwinding with a hobby like knitting or painting. Whatever your answer may be, **show that you are not afraid of stress and are actually pretty good at handling it**. Demonstrate that **you treat stress as positive**

rather than negative, and that helps you do your job better.

9. What are your accomplishments in life?

When asked about your accomplishments, do not be a case of false modesty. Be proud and brag when you have something to brag about. Mention the company policy you had implemented which increased productivity, and effectively cut down on precious work hours wasted on a particular task. Impress your interviewer with awards and recognitions which you have rightfully earned both in the workplace and outside.

Awards for sports or arts achievements that have no relation to your line of work are still important accomplishments that should not be brushed aside. Furthermore, accomplishments are not always measurable or can be validated by a piece of paper or a medal. Accomplishments in life can also include starting a family or building a home.

10. What are your strengths?

Employers are usually looking for people who possess certain positive traits. **Creativity** is highly valued in the workplace. Being able to think outside the box and innovate is encouraged in order for a company to progress. **Communication skills** are useful because being able to communicate your ideas will allow those ideas to actually come to life. Determination and hard work are also important when looking at prospective employees, as well as a highly positive attitude towards everything. Also, elaborate on these strengths and demonstrate how you are, for example, a highly creative person. Think of the instances in your career wherein you exhibited creativity in accomplishing a particular task.

11. What are your weaknesses?

It is never good to admit to any weakness, but do not say you have no weaknesses either. Everyone has weaknesses, but the people you look up to are usually working on these weaknesses and using these to improve themselves further. Show that you are one of these people. For example, you could say that you have been a procrastinator, but you took a seminar on time management and are currently using a daily planner to organize your work day.

Another usual trick is to state weaknesses that are actually strengths. You can say that you sometimes forget to take breaks because you like finishing everything you start in one go. Lastly, you may also state weaknesses that have no relation to the job you are applying for. If you are a graphic designer, then it would not be a disadvantage if you happen to not be very good at Math or statistical analysis.

12. What are your skills?

Know the job description and qualifications. What did it say in the job ad? Take note of the skills they specified and make sure that your own skills fit their requirements. Some skills may be job-specific and unique to that particular line of work. For example, accountants should have great attention to detail, problem solving and analytic skills.

Customer service representatives should have strong oral communication skills, and can tolerate stress and pressure. Other general key skills that employers look for are being proactive or having initiative, planning and organization skills, presentation skills and leadership skills. Depending on the job, technological and technical skills are also an advantage, such as using word processing software or creating presentation slides.

13. Why did you leave your last job?

It is really the most obvious reason why you are at a job interview—because you are looking for another job. **Never give any negative feedback on your company, your boss or your work.** Do not state any grievances and bad blood which you may have. This shows poor taste and might turn off the interviewer. You can instead say that the company was going a certain direction and your team wished to go a different way, including you.

Make it sound like the feeling was shared with other people in the company to show that you were not a special case, which might trigger certain alarms. Say that although you enjoyed your stay at the company, you wanted to explore instead other opportunities outside in order to advance your career.

14. Could you explain these gaps in your employment?

You resumé might have long periods in between employment. Employers might think that you were unemployable at this time, and had trouble landing a job. Explain these gaps and state good reasons for them. Perhaps you had to take a break to focus on settling down with your new family or moving to a new state. Maybe, you have a small online business on the side wherein you needed time to set up and get things going.

Possibly, you pursued further degree studies in order to

expand your knowledge about your industry. Make your reasons related to family or business that show that you were attending to other responsibilities other than work.

15. Could you explain why you did not stay at this job for longer?

In your resumé, you might have jobs that lasted for only a short time. Elaborate that these were choices, rather than the result of not being able to hold on to one job long enough—be it from getting fired or from sheer incompetence. Maybe, other opportunities elsewhere presented itself, and you chose to seize those opportunities before it was too late. Having gone through several jobs can also be presented as an advantage because you have been exposed to different companies and cultures and have a broader perspective on your line of work than someone who has been with the same company for so many years.

16. What would these references say about you?

You may have been asked to provide a list of references for your prospective employer to use in doing your background check or in getting recommendations. Try not to elaborate too much on your answer to this one. The shorter and simpler your answer is, the less likely you would say anything that might conflict with what your references might say.

Remember how they have positively described you in the past and repeat that to the interviewer. Although at the onset, make sure that the references you give would say nothing but praises about you, and really do know you very well and have worked with you in the past.

9

KEEP A POSITIVE MIND

Recall the beginning of this book: let us begin at the end. Visualize yourself at your dream job. How do you feel? What positive changes would this new work bring to your life?

Imagine how it would be like to start your day and head off to work at your new office. What are the sights and sounds that you encounter? Remember these sensations. Think of your new desk at your new cubicle or, even better, your new corner office with that beautiful view of the cityscape. Imagine what it would be like walking through the hallways of the swanky building that is your company's headquarters. Say hello to the colleagues you encounter along the way. Think of how board meetings would go and the many ideas, concepts and plans that you wish to share with the board.

Say hello to your team, the team that will help you execute and make all these plans a wonderful reality. Imagine further some more, how it would be like to sit at your desk, with a cup of coffee, reading through the daily accomplishment and progress reports prepared by your team, and seeing the contributions you have made to the company creating a positive effect. Knowing that this is the end goal will certainly put you in a good mood, and stay positive as you go through the rigors of job hunting and interviewing because this will all be worth it in the end.

Another technique you could do to be positive right before the interview is to give yourself a pep talk. You may find yourself feeling a little bit silly about this, but it works. Repeat your strengths and skills so you remember them during your interview. Recall your work experience and tell yourself that with these as weapons (qualifications), you will conquer this battle (the job interview) easily. Just psyching yourself up and giving yourself a confidence boost will easily change your aura. If you believe in yourself hard enough, so will other people. Other people recognize confidence and they always respond positively to it. They also love optimistic people and these usually produce good results in the long run.

AFTERWORD

Now that you know all the things to be successful in getting a job, you've got to just get out there and get into action, if you haven't already. Continue to use this book as a guide and refer back to it for reminders of how to be successful during your job search, application process, and interview to get that job you desire!

I wish you much success and happiness in your career!

www.ingramcontent.com/pod-product-compliance
Lightning Source LLC
Chambersburg PA
CBHW070037040426
42333CB00040B/1711